MAKING A CITY
SMART

BY BETHANY ONSGARD

CONTENT CONSULTANT
Xuan (Sharon) Di, PhD
Assistant Professor of Civil Engineering
and Engineering Mechanics
Columbia University

Cover image: Workers use smart technology to
monitor road conditions and traffic at a traffic
management center.

Core Library

An Imprint of Abdo Publishing
abdopublishing.com

abdopublishing.com

Published by Abdo Publishing, a division of ABDO, PO Box 398166, Minneapolis, Minnesota 55439. Copyright © 2019 by Abdo Consulting Group, Inc. International copyrights reserved in all countries. No part of this book may be reproduced in any form without written permission from the publisher. Core Library™ is a trademark and logo of Abdo Publishing.

Printed in the United States of America, North Mankato, Minnesota
042018
092018

Cover Photos: Evgenya Novozhenina/Sputnik/AP Images
Interior Photos: Evgenya Novozhenina/Sputnik/AP Images, 1; Sean Pavone/Shutterstock Images, 4–5, 43; qnb/Imaginechina/AP Images, 7; Shutterstock Images, 9; Sundry Photography/ Shutterstock Images, 12–13; Lino Marcel Mirgeler/picture-alliance/dpa/AP Images, 15; Red Line Editorial, 17, 40; Silvia Flores/The Fresno Bee/AP Images, 20–21; Eric Risberg/AP Images, 24; Miroslav Chaloupka/CTK/AP Images, 26; Laura Emmons/The Daily Times/AP Images, 28–29; Zacharie Scheurer/AP Images, 32, 45; Jorge Salcedo/Shutterstock Images, 34; John Alex Maguire/ REX/Shutterstock, 36–37

Editor: Maddie Spalding
Imprint Designer: Maggie Villaume
Series Design Direction: Claire Vanden Branden

Library of Congress Control Number: 2017962643

Publisher's Cataloging-in-Publication Data

Names: Onsgard, Bethany, author.
Title: Making a city smart / by Bethany Onsgard.
Description: Minneapolis, Minnesota : Abdo Publishing, 2019. | Series: Inside modern cities | Includes online resources and index.
Identifiers: ISBN 9781532114816 (lib.bdg.) | ISBN 9781532154645 (ebook)
Subjects: LCSH: Engineering design--Juvenile literature. | Technology--Juvenile literature. | City planning--Juvenile literature. | Cities and towns--Juvenile literature. Architecture and technology--Juvenile literature.
Classification: DDC 624.023--dc23

CONTENTS

WHAT MAKES A CITY SMART?

Boston, Massachusetts, is one of the most walkable cities in the United States. The city has many walking paths. Boston's government is also committed to making roads safe for all commuters.

In 2015 Boston's mayor announced the Vision Zero project. The Vision Zero project is a plan to bring the number of traffic-related deaths in Boston down to zero. The city aims to do this by 2030. As part of this project, the city set up video cameras and sensors along its busiest streets. The magnetic sensors are in the road. They are made up of coils of wire.

In Boston, Massachusetts, officials are exploring how to make intersections and crosswalks safer.

An electric current runs through the wires. When a car drives over a sensor, the flow of the current changes. The sensors can measure the speed, number, and size of vehicles that pass over them.

Cameras and sensors on Boston's streets collect data on how drivers, cyclists, and pedestrians interact. This data is sent to computer systems on poles at each intersection. The systems analyze the data. The city uses this data to make the roads safer. City workers are improving crosswalks along busy streets. This includes making crosswalk markings more visible to drivers.

Boston is not the only city to collect data.

CAMERAS AND SENSORS

Many devices and machines have cameras or sensors. Some cars have sensors. The sensors tell drivers when air pressure in the tires is low. Some watches have sensors. The sensors track calories burned and steps taken. Some refrigerators have cameras. People can view the contents of their refrigerator from their phones. This allows them to see what groceries they need.

Smart lampposts in Shanghai, China, can charge electric vehicles, report on traffic conditions, and perform many other tasks.

Most cities monitor air pollution, traffic patterns, and other statistics. Smart cities use this data to improve the lives of their residents. Smart cities run efficiently. They direct resources toward people who need them most. They also use data to predict and solve problems. They share this data with residents to keep them informed.

WHY BE SMART?

Smart cities conserve resources and save money. For example, some cities install smart lighting. In 2009 Los Angeles, California, began replacing streetlights with LED lights. LED lights use less energy than traditional lighting. They also last longer. By 2016 nearly 80 percent of the city's lights had been replaced. The city is saving nearly $9 million each year in electricity costs. These types of projects save cities both energy and money.

Residents in smart cities can save money as well. For example, some homes use smart meters. Smart meters monitor energy and water use. This can encourage people to conserve resources. People can see how much energy or water they are using. The more they conserve, the more money they save.

SMART TECHNOLOGY

Smart lighting and smart meters are examples of smart technology. Smart technology collects information from

LED streetlights help cities such as Los Angeles, California, save money.

the environment. It also responds to that information. Smart technology is often connected to the internet.

Cities have been collecting data for many years. Smart technology and internet connectivity have helped improve data collection. Data is stored on computers. Other devices can access this information through the internet.

Data storage has become more affordable as more people rely on it. Sensors have also become more affordable. This makes it cheaper and easier for cities and residents to monitor problems. Advances in technology also help smart cities develop.

STRAIGHT TO THE
SOURCE

In 2015 more than 70 US cities competed in the US Department of Transportation's Smart Cities Challenge. Each city submitted a problem it faces as well as potential solutions. Pittsburgh, Pennsylvania, outlined the goals for its plan:

> *The City of Pittsburgh maintains 40,000 streetlights on the more than 2,400 lane miles [3,860 km] of city, state, and county-owned roadways. In 2011, the City of Pittsburgh began converting streetlights in primary corridors and in neighborhood business districts to LED. . . . The LED conversion project will provide for significant energy savings, increased safety and mobility, and an array of sensor data. . . . The City expects to save approximately 60%, or $650,000, on annual energy costs.*

> Source: "USDOT Smart City Challenge: City of Pittsburgh Vision Narrative." *US Department of Transportation.* US Department of Transportation, 2015. Web. Accessed November 17, 2017.

What's the Big Idea?
Take a close look at this passage. What solution does the city of Pittsburgh outline for its energy problem? What are other ways the city might have solved this problem?

SMART CITIES AND HEALTH

Smart cities aim to meet many goals. One goal is to improve residents' health. Governments work to keep a city's air and water clean. Emissions from vehicles and factories can pollute the air. This can make the air unsafe to breathe.

AIR QUALITY

The city of Oakland, California, is home to a major port. The port is located along San Francisco Bay. It connects US railroads to international trade routes. Many trucks pass through the city each day. These vehicles emit pollutants. The pollutants include soot and

Cities such as Oakland, California, use smart technology to keep residents healthy.

SMART LIGHT BULBS

In 2017 the government of Louisville, Kentucky, created a program. The program alerts residents to poor air quality. The city monitors air quality. It shares that information with residents through IFTTT. IFTTT is a free internet service. People in homes with smart light bulbs can sign up for alerts. These light bulbs are connected to the city's air quality data. The light bulbs turn red when the air quality is unsafe. This warns residents not to go outside. Residents without smart light bulbs can receive text messages. The messages give them information about the city's air quality.

nitrogen dioxide. Soot is a black powder. Nitrogen dioxide is a harmful gas. Because of this pollution, some neighborhoods in Oakland have very poor air quality.

Oakland partnered with Google in 2015. Google equipped its Street View cars with air quality monitors. These cars drive all around the world to take photos for Google's mapping service. In Oakland, the cars drove around

Some cities have air quality monitoring stations, which measure the amount of pollutants in the air.

neighborhoods. They collected air quality data for one year.

The monitors measured the amounts of chemicals in the air. One type of monitor collects air samples. It shoots a laser beam through the samples. The monitor measures how much light the air particles have absorbed. This tells researchers how much soot is in the air.

Another type of monitor shines light between two mirrors. The presence of nitrogen dioxide causes a shift in the light stream. A detector inside the monitor measures the shift. This shows how much nitrogen dioxide is in the sample.

Measurements from these monitors helped locate areas in Oakland with poor air quality. The Environmental Defense Fund, a nonprofit group, created maps based on this data. The maps showed which neighborhoods needed the most help fighting air pollution.

WATER QUALITY

Air pollutants also affect water. They make water more acidic. High acidity in lakes and other bodies of water can affect animal health. It can reduce fish and marine animal populations. It can also cause algae to grow in water. Algae is a type of plant. Large patches of

AIR QUALITY INDEX

Numerical Value (particle concentrations)	Levels of Health Concern	Color
0 – 50	Good	Green
51 – 100	Moderate	Yellow
101 – 150	Unhealthy for Sensitive People	Orange
151 – 200	Unhealthy	Red
201 – 300	Very Unhealthy	Purple
301 – 500	Hazardous	Maroon

Local governments often use a measurement called an Air Quality Index (AQI). The AQI uses colors to show the concentration of particles in the air. The above chart shows what each color means. How do you think smart cities could use this information?

algae that grow in acidic water are called harmful algal blooms. They produce toxins. The toxins can cause problems such as skin irritations.

Many cities are exploring technologies to better measure water quality. One such city is Tilburg in the Netherlands. Water quality sensors were installed around a harbor near the city's center. The sensors measure the level of acidity in the water. This helps the city determine how safe the water is for swimming or other activities.

HEALTH CODE VIOLATIONS

Data collection can also help prevent restaurant health code violations. Health code violations occur when food isn't cooked or prepared properly. This can cause food poisoning or other illnesses.

The city of Chicago, Illinois, has more than 15,000 restaurants.

Only 36 health inspectors are assigned to check on these restaurants. In 2015 the city's data team created an algorithm. The algorithm predicts which restaurants may have health code violations in the future. This helps the city stay ahead of violations. A data team looked at how many violations each restaurant had in the past. They also looked at how long each restaurant had been open. Restaurants that have been in business for a long time are less likely to have problems. Another factor the team considered was the weather. Keeping food refrigerated helps make sure it is safe to eat. But keeping food cool is more difficult when the weather is warm. For this reason, health code violations happen more often when it's warm. Health inspectors checked in more often on restaurants that were predicted to have a health code violation. This ensured restaurants followed health codes.

CHAPTER THREE

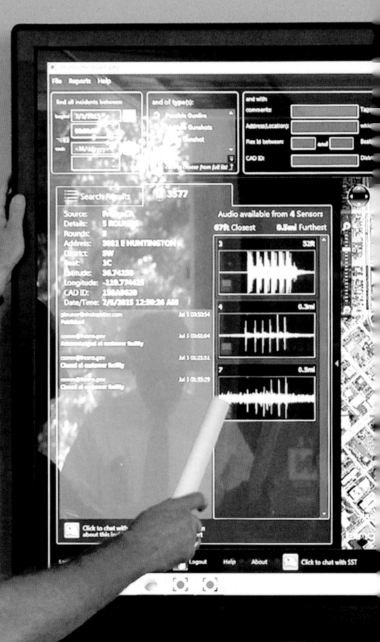

SMART CITIES AND SAFETY

O ne of a city's biggest concerns is keeping its residents safe. Cities have police departments, fire departments, and city planners. These people create plans for emergencies and natural disasters. Smart cities use data to keep their residents safe.

LAW ENFORCEMENT

New technologies can help law enforcement respond more quickly to crime. Sensors attached to buildings can track gunshots. They analyze sound waves. This helps them pinpoint the exact location where a gun was fired.

A city's law enforcement can use sensors to collect evidence and identify where crime might happen.

Drones may also help law enforcement. Drones are aircraft that fly without a pilot. They can scope out potentially dangerous situations. They can send video footage and other data to officials. Some smartphone apps allow residents to send alerts to law enforcement when a crime or medical emergency happens. The app can record video or audio of the scene. Police officers can use this as evidence.

Smart cities can also use data to predict and prevent crime. Many US cities have launched programs with a technology called PredPol. PredPol is short for "predictive policing." PredPol divides a region of the city into boxes. A computer program analyzes the types of crimes that have happened in each box. It looks at when and where these crimes happened. The program uses this data to identify hot spots. Hot spots are areas where crime is predicted to happen again. Police can focus their attention on these hot spots to help prevent crime.

NATURAL DISASTERS

Many of the world's cities are vulnerable to natural disasters. Coastal cities may be vulnerable to floods, hurricanes, and tsunamis. Some cities and communities are vulnerable to earthquakes. One common problem after a natural disaster is a power outage. Smart infrastructure can help solve this problem.

In San Francisco, California, experts are working on an early-warning system that can detect earthquakes and slow down trains before the ground starts shaking.

Smart infrastructure is equipped with sensors. The sensors are connected to computer systems. A city's infrastructure includes power grids as well as gas and water networks. When a natural disaster happens, the infrastructure can tell the system where outages are occurring. Smart infrastructure can also share energy resources. This way, the city can divert energy from less important uses to help restore power.

FIRE SAFETY

In many cities, fire departments give out free smoke detectors. But people usually must request them. In 2015 New Orleans, Louisiana, used a program to predict which houses were most at risk for fire. Officials studied the history of fires in the city. They identified households that included young children and the elderly. These populations have the greatest risk of dying in a fire. Children may not be able to escape by themselves. Elderly people may have illnesses or

SMART METERS

In 2012 Hurricane Sandy hit the East Coast of the United States. It caused power outages in many states. A power company called Pepco used its network of smart meters to find where power outages occurred. Smart meters measure the amount of electricity used by a household. They communicate this information to a power company. After power was restored, Pepco didn't need to send a crew or call residents to determine which households needed service. Instead, the company simply communicated with the smart meters.

disabilities that make it hard for them to escape. This
data was used by the New Orleans Fire Department.
They installed free smoke detectors in the most
at-risk households.

Fire departments also perform building inspections
to make sure buildings are fire resistant. Many fire
departments have limited resources. This means they
need to prioritize which buildings to inspect. Data
collection can help them predict which buildings are
most at risk of fire. Analysts in Atlanta, Georgia, created
a computer model to predict future fires. The model
analyzed the location, age, and size of buildings in

the city. The model found that large buildings with many rooms had the highest risk of fire. The model predicted 71 percent of fires. This made it 2.5 times more effective than the old model many fire departments were using.

Smart technology can help after fires start, too. When firefighters arrive at a building, they need to know what's inside. Computer records can show them the building's layout. Sensors inside can track where smoke and heat have reached. Firefighters can use this information to put out the fire.

FURTHER EVIDENCE

Chapter Three explores how smart cities can improve safety measures. What was one of the main points of this chapter? What key evidence supports this point? Read the article at the website below. Does the information on the website support this point? Or does it present new evidence?

SMART CITIES VERSUS MOTHER NATURE
abdocorelibrary.com/making-a-city-smart

SMART TRANSPORT

Each day many people commute within a city. Students travel to school. Adults travel to work. They commute by car, bike, or bus or on foot. Some cities use smart technology to make commutes quicker and easier.

SMART TRAFFIC

Traffic is a problem in many cities. There may be traffic jams during high-traffic times. Smart cities can address this problem through smart traffic lights. Smart traffic lights use artificial intelligence (AI) and sensors. This equipment responds to traffic conditions.

Sensors and cameras can collect data to help improve traffic conditions.

SELF-DRIVING CARS

Self-driving cars operate without a driver. They use detailed maps of streets and traffic signs. Computers within self-driving cars gather and access information about road conditions. This information could be accessed from city infrastructure and from other cars. Vehicle-to-vehicle (V2V) technology allows communication between cars. Cars can communicate location and speed. Vehicle-to-infrastructure (V2I) technology allows communication between cars and infrastructure. Cars can share data with traffic lights and other infrastructure. These technologies will allow self-driving cars to avoid traffic and improve rider safety.

AI uses a computer to perform tasks normally done by humans. These tasks include making decisions and interpreting data.

Pittsburgh is one city that uses smart traffic lights. In 2012 smart traffic lights were placed at some intersections in the city. A computer at each intersection is linked to a camera or radar device. This device detects oncoming traffic. The computer monitors the traffic. It builds a timing plan.

A timing plan is a decision about how long a red or green light should be displayed. The computers also communicate with each other about oncoming and expected traffic. Together, these computers develop a plan. They respond to and predict traffic conditions. They coordinate the smart lights based on this data. If traffic going one way is heavy, then the light might change to green more quickly for cars going in that direction. This can prevent traffic jams.

In Pittsburgh, smart lights have reduced travel time by 25 percent. This technology will cover one-third of the city by 2020. Other US cities also are using or plan to use smart lights to reduce traffic.

SMART BUSES

Public transportation is available in many large cities. Smart cities make public transportation more efficient. For example, the smart traffic light system in Los Angeles, California, responds to bus schedules. City buses drive in their own lanes. Magnetic sensors in the

Some smart cities, such as Paris, France, are experimenting with self-driving buses.

roads detect buses. The computer network adjusts traffic lights. It gives green lights to buses running behind schedule.

Smart cities also work to improve safety measures on public transportation. A company called Mobileye developed technology for this purpose. Its buses each have four cameras. The cameras focus on the driver's blind spots. A computer uses the cameras to identify pedestrians and predict collisions. The computer alerts the driver through a dashboard screen. This gives the driver enough reaction time to prevent an accident.

BIKE LANES

In many cities, cyclists share the road with cars. This can make biking dangerous. But in some cities, governments add special bike lanes. Lanes that are planned well can help keep cyclists safe. Smart technology can help cities build safe bike lanes.

In the past, some cities used manual counting to determine where people biked most often. Government workers stood by the side of a road. They counted each cyclist. Now, in some smart cities, technology does the counting. This is the case in San Francisco. Workers installed

PERSPECTIVES
WI-FI ON BUSES

For years, many people passed the time on mass transit by reading a book or a newspaper. But now more mass transit systems offer free Wi-Fi. People can use their commute time to catch up on a favorite show or browse social media, among other things. This has made mass transit a more enjoyable experience to many commuters. Bus drivers can also benefit from Wi-Fi access. Many buses have surveillance cameras that use an internet connection. These cameras help prevent crime. They can also provide evidence in criminal investigations.

Visible lane markings and barriers can help protect cyclists on busy streets.

road sensors in San Francisco. These sensors track the number of bikes that pass on the road. This system is more accurate than manual counting. But many cities still do not collect such data. This can make it difficult for a city to assess whether roads are accessible to bikers. San Francisco acts as an example that other smart cities may follow.

Smart cities can also access data from biking apps. Cyclists often track their routes on apps such as Strava. City planners can use this information to map where people are biking. They can see which routes cyclists prefer to use. Then they can create safer bike lanes in those areas. Making lane markings more visible and widening bike lanes can make them safer.

STRAIGHT TO THE
SOURCE

In a 2014 US Department of Transportation report, researchers described trends emerging in smart transportation:

> The infrastructure of a smart and connected city is increasingly a system of systems. . . . Transportation systems interface with employment, residential, healthcare, utility, and city services systems. . . . In a vehicle-to-infrastructure (V2I) or vehicle-to-vehicle (V2V) system, connected vehicles will continuously broadcast location, speed, and other data. This will give traffic management systems real-time data on traffic conditions that are far more detailed and accurate than data available today.

> Source: Matthew Cuddy, et al. "The Smart/Connected City and Its Implications for Connected Transportation—White Paper." *US Department of Transportation*. US Department of Transportation, October 14, 2014. Web. Accessed December 28, 2017.

Consider Your Audience

Adapt this passage for a different audience, such as your teacher or friends. Write a blog post conveying this same information for the new audience. How does your post differ from the original text and why?